ACTING FOR NATURE

ACTING FOR NATURE

What Young People Around the World
Have Done to Protect the Environment

Sneed B. Collard III and Action for Nature
Illustrated by Carl Dennis Buell

Heyday Books
Berkeley, California

To all young people throughout the world who strive to make the world a better place for humans and for nature.

A portion of the proceeds from the sale of this book will go toward supporting the programs of Action for Nature.

© 2000 by Action for Nature

Library of Congress Cataloging in Publication Data:

Collard, Sneed B.
    Acting for nature : what young people around the world have done to protect the environment / Sneed B. Collard ; illustrations by Carl Dennis Buell.
        p.   cm.
    Summary: Describes the efforts of young people to protect the environment in their communities in different countries around the world.
        ISBN 1-890771-24-4 (pbk.)
        1. Child environmentalists Case studies Juvenile literature. [1. Environmentalists. 2. Environmental protection. 3. Conservation of natural resources.] I. Buell, Carl Dennis, ill. II. Title.
    GE195.5.C65   1999   2000
    333.7'2'0922—dc21
                                                                    99-39670
                                                                    CIP

Cover Art: Carl Dennis Buell
Cover and Interior Design: Rebecca LeGates
Printing and Binding: Publishers Press, Salt Lake City, Utah
Printed on recycled paper.

Orders, inquiries, and correspondence should be addressed to:

Heyday Books
P.O. Box 9145, Berkeley, CA 94709
510/549-3564; Fax 510/549-1889
heyday@heydaybooks.com

Printed in the United States of America

10 9 8 7 6 5 4 3 2 1

CONTENTS

INTRODUCTION

In the slums of Nairobi, Kenya, jacaranda and acacia trees now line the streets where ten years ago, there was only mud and cement. In London, England, an ancient forest still stands where government agencies had planned to construct a four-lane expressway. And in the Atlantic Ocean, hundreds of loggerhead sea turtles swim free, when at one time, they were sentenced to certain death. None of these small miracles would have happened without the caring action and dedication of young people.

Many young people throughout the world recognize that our planet is in trouble. They've read the headlines and seen for themselves that overpopulation, pollution, poor planning, and greed are leading to a wide range of environmental disasters. Faced with problems of such magnitude, many people feel powerless to change things and give up hope. But not the young men and women in this book.

The following pages tell the stories of young people from eleven different countries who looked at the problems in their communities and decided to do something to help. Some worked alone, while others enlisted friends, family, and community members. Some tackled immediate problems, while others focused on long-term goals. None of their tasks were easy, and most faced serious obstacles. But these young men and women used their creativity, intelligence, diplomacy, and persistence to change their world for the better. They also used their greatest weapons: their hearts.

We hope you enjoy these stories. Even more, we hope they help you discover your own unique gifts and passions, and inspire you to help protect this incredible planet we all share.

WALKING FOR
WILDLIFE

One hundred years ago, on a 3.6-hectare (nine-acre) industrial site near Horncastle in Lincolnshire, England, the crackling of burning coal and the shouts of workers filled the air. Men dug clay from a huge, deep pit and hauled it up to other workers, who hand-kneaded the clay until it became soft. When the clay reached the right consistency, the men threw it into standard-sized molds and left it to dry outside for about a week. Then, they moved the raw bricks into drying sheds for another two weeks. After drying, the bricks—35,000 at a time—were baked in a large coal-fired kiln. Horse-drawn wagons hauled them off by the thousands to build houses, farms, and churches throughout the area.

The clay pits had been in operation since the sixteenth century. While the brickyard stayed open, it provided a good living for dozens of people, but like most industrial sites, it had been cleared of trees and most other living things. In 1905, however, the brickyard closed. Within a few years, trees and shrubs began to reclaim the site. Animals joined them. A family of foxes crept in to hunt mice and voles. Rabbits, gray squirrels, and hedgehogs made their homes among the new shrubs and crumbling buildings. The old clay pits filled with water and began to attract geese, ducks, and other birds. Then, in 1981, a family of humans moved in: the Fawcett family, consisting of two parents and three children, including three-month-old Caroline.

From the start, the family felt at home on the old industrial site. Caroline's parents had a keen interest in the history of

1

the region and set about restoring the kiln and other surviving buildings. But Caroline was too young to help with the frequently hazardous restoration work. Instead, she became drawn to the plants and animals that shared her new home. She learned to identify ash, chestnut, and willow trees, many of which were over 100 years old. She delighted in discovering the fresh footprints of water fowl, voles, and foxes beside the pond.

Caroline formed a special bond with a family of barn owls that nested in a nearby ash tree. At dawn and dusk, Caroline's pulse would race as she caught a glimpse of one of these silent hunters gliding across the backlit sky with a vole or mouse dangling from its talons. Eager to discover what and how much the owls had eaten, she often took time to dissect and study the pellets— the gobs of hair and bone that owls regurgitate after their meals—left behind by the owls.

The more she learned about the plants and animals around her home, however, the more Caroline recognized that improvements could be made for their well-being—and the more she wanted to share her world with other people. At age six, she decided that while her parents restored the buildings of the brickyard, she would set about restoring the land as a nature preserve.

Caroline, with her father's assistance, began by pulling fallen trees from the two ponds that now occupied the site. Since the brick factory had closed, the land had been used by a tenant farmer, and years of household garbage had been tipped down the banks of the ponds. Caroline cleared away as much of this as she could, making the ponds more attractive to people and safer for wildlife.

Next, Caroline began constructing a nature trail through the preserve. She replanted native wildflowers and wrote a guide to the trees, birds, and other points of interest along the trail. From the Royal Society for the Protection of Birds, she obtained instructions for building bird and bat boxes. With help from her father, she nailed together a number of designs for different bird and bat species and hung them on trees near the nature trail.

Caroline regularly called on experts to help her choose what plants and animals to bring into the preserve and what steps to take to improve the habitat for wildlife. Soon, local school groups, birdwatchers, and other people heard about Caroline's work and began visiting the site on a regular basis.

One day, however, fate pushed Caroline's efforts in a new direction. After morning tea, Caroline decided to go for a walk. She passed a bush and smelled the familiar musky scent a fox had left there during the night. Walking along a hedgerow, she spotted her neighbor, Mr. Lindley, with his dog, Jimmy. Mr. Lindley seemed upset and told Caroline that, while out walking along the road, he had encountered a dead owl.

Caroline felt her heart leap to her throat, and she hurried out to the roadside. There, with its downy feathers quivering in the breeze, lay the broken body of a dead barn owl. Caroline's eyes filled with tears as she recognized it as one of this year's fledglings from her own barn owl family.

Unfortunately, the barn owl's death was just one of many in Great Britain. Barn owls hunt mice, voles, and other small rodents that frequent meadows, feedyards, and other open areas. One of the best hunting grounds for the birds, however, is in the taller grasses along Britain's roadsides. Here, they often swoop low to find and capture their prey. Unfortunately, in doing so, between 3,000–5,000 owls are struck and killed by cars every year.

Seeing the birds' plight firsthand spurred Caroline to begin learning more about barn owls and how she might help these graceful creatures. The Hawk Trust, a conservation group to which Caroline belonged, had published a pamphlet about owl conservation. Reading it, Caroline learned that many places where barn owls hunted were disappearing. Traditionally, for instance, many owls hunted along hedgerows—long rows of shrubs that separated fields on farms and estates in England. During the past decades, however, farmers had been cutting down their hedgerows to squeeze in more crops. In the past forty years, 140,000 miles of hedgerows had been destroyed and with them, the homes and hunting grounds of many animals, including the barn owl.

Caroline decided that one thing she could do to help was to collect signatures to urge the government to conserve and replant hedgerows and other grass strips throughout Great Britain. Accompanied by her mother, Caroline visited nearby towns, talked to shopkeepers and their customers about the plight of the barn owls, and asked people to sign her petition. She also asked her teachers, relatives, and neighbors to sign. Moved by Caroline's sincerity, over 400 people signed the petition, and Caroline presented it in person to Britain's Minister of the Environment. She followed this up by writing hundreds of letters to newspapers and influential people, urging the conservation of hedgerows and grass strips.

Caroline also recognized that she could improve the brickyard's own owl habitat. She called British Telecom and asked if

> At dawn and dusk, Caroline's pulse would race as she caught a glimpse of one of these silent hunters gliding across the backlit sky with a vole or mouse dangling from its talons.

they might erect a telephone pole on her family's land so that they could mount an owl nesting box. The giant phone company not only agreed to put in one pole, but three! Soon, in addition to the barn owl family, families of little owls and tawny owls moved onto her site.

In 1989, when she was eight years old, Caroline's activities earned her invitations from England's Ministry of Environment, the House of Lords, and the House of Commons to discuss environmental matters with ministers and members of Parliament. Over the next two years, she was featured on several television documentaries and won conservation awards from the Royal Society for the Protection of Birds, W.A.T.C.H., and the Ford Motor Company.

But Caroline was just warming up.

As she continued to make improvements to her own nature preserve and learned more about conservation work, she became acutely aware of the need for two important assets: publicity and money. Publicity was essential in making the public aware of conservation issues. Money was needed to actually improve ways of doing things. Funding, especially, had always been an issue for Caroline. She had paid for most of her projects with her own money, and she realized that if it was hard for her to make ends meet, it must also be hard for conservation organizations.

In the summer of 1990, at age nine, Caroline and her family were visiting different historic sites in England, and they camped

in a place called St. Bees Head in Cumbria. There, Caroline noticed a lot of people setting off with hiking boots and backpacks. Talking with some of the hikers, she learned that St. Bees Head was the starting point for the coast-to-coast walk that led across England. After watching a number of hikers set off on the 339-kilometer (210-mile) trail, Caroline turned to her parents and said, "I want to do that next year." Furthermore, she decided she would use the walk to raise money for conservation projects.

After gathering a number of sponsors, Caroline and her mom set off on the coast-to-coast walk the following August. Every morning, Caroline's dad dropped them off at the starting point for that day, and she and her mom walked between thirteen and twenty-nine kilometers (eight to eighteen miles). At night, they slept in the family's camper van, which her dad drove from place to place along their route.

Each day offered Caroline a fresh, vivid experience that she would never forget. One day, she and her mom became enthralled with a gold ringed dragonfly laying its eggs in a hillside stream. Another day, descending a hill in a beating rainstorm, Caroline discovered a spring burbling out of the ground. "It was bubbling like a boiling pan, and looking into it was like looking into a bottomless black hole," she recalled.

In each county she passed through, reporters interviewed her about her walk and her thoughts on conservation. If people driving by spotted her, they often stopped and put money in her donation box. One day, when hiking through Yorkshire, she and her mom passed a lady and her sheep dog next to the road. The woman had packed a lunch and had come to give them a picnic in Caroline's honor.

The walk took Caroline five weeks. As she neared the end of her journey at Robin Hood's Bay, she was suddenly confronted by a marching band complete with majorettes, a man dressed as Captain Cook, and a throng of townspeople. Caroline was shocked. Then "Captain Cook" told her that he, the band, and townspeople had all come out to congratulate her on finishing her walk! As Caroline stared in amazement at the commotion

> Caroline felt her heart leap to her throat, and she hurried out to the roadside. There, with its downy feathers quivering in the breeze, lay the broken body of a dead barn owl.

surrounding her, a town crier summoned all the townspeople to come celebrate Caroline's campaign. Caroline (and Captain Cook) officially ended her journey by splashing her feet in the North Sea, and the Lord Mayor met Caroline and presented her with a certificate of achievement.

All told, Caroline's walk raised £2,200 (about $4,000), which she distributed to different conservation groups in England. She made a special donation of £500 to the Owl Centre at Muncaster Castle in Cumbria, and they used the money to build an aviary for breeding endangered European brown fish owls. They named the facility The Caroline Fawcett Aviary.

After the walk, Caroline continued pursuing her conservation efforts. She built a "hide" on her preserve, a place where people could go to watch birds without disturbing them. She also improved the trails around the preserve to ensure that they were accessible by wheelchair. As people got to know her, they also began bringing Caroline injured birds, and she worked with vets to learn how to care for them.

When she turned twelve, Caroline convinced a local company to donate a small trailer to her, and she transformed it into a conservation display. On the outside, she painted a mural of Britain's wildlife and habitats. On the inside, she developed an educational display focusing on the conservation of barn owls. Creating two characters—Barney the Barn Owl and Victoria Vole—as guides, she painted posters that illustrated the plight of barn owls and described their biology. She also created a workbench where children could dissect owl pellets. After completing the displays, she and her father took it to schools, libraries, and other public places and guided thousands of children through it to teach them to appreciate and conserve Britain's natural resources.

As her efforts became better known, Caroline continued to accrue awards and honors. When she got older, though, she began to remove herself from the spotlight, recognizing that conservation is not a matter of being a star, but of working together with other people. Now, as she prepares to study computers and information technology, she no longer has as much time to devote to the preserve as she would like. However, she hopes that her efforts have inspired other youngsters and adults to initiate their own efforts.

"A lot of suffering of wildlife has been caused through ignorance," she says. "Showing people a better way to live alongside nature will go a long way to redressing environmental problems. You don't need to find somewhere that is special—just care for what you see. Then, by your example, others will learn. It's a bit like rolling a snowball. It gets bigger and bigger as you go along."

THE POWER OF INFORMATION

When twelve-year-old Andrew Holleman read the letter, he felt sick to his stomach. The letter stated that a developer was planning to transform six hectares (sixteen acres) of wildlands in Chelmsford, Massachusetts, into a new subdivision with roads, drainage pipes, sewers, and 180 houses. This development would destroy one of Andrew's favorite places on earth.

A fishing pole balanced across his shoulder, Andrew had often followed a dirt footpath into the local wildlands area. Here, he would walk underneath towering white pines and pass enormous rocks left by glaciers ten thousand years before. After dropping his fishing line into a clear brook, he would study the cattails along the water's edge for a glimpse of a great blue heron or a wood turtle. Sometimes a large-mouth bass would gently tug at his line, and other times it wouldn't, but this spot always gave Andrew a chance to be alone with his thoughts and take a break from school, baseball, and the swim team.

Now, however, Andrew's special place was in danger.

After overcoming his initial outrage at the developer's plan, Andrew started thinking about ways he could save his sanctuary. Before he began, he knew he needed more information, so he visited the local library. With the help of a librarian, Andrew found information on the Hatch Act, a Massachusetts law that protected wetlands from being removed, dredged, or filled in. Andrew also located a copy of the town's master plan and learned that it classified over half of the threatened property as wetlands.

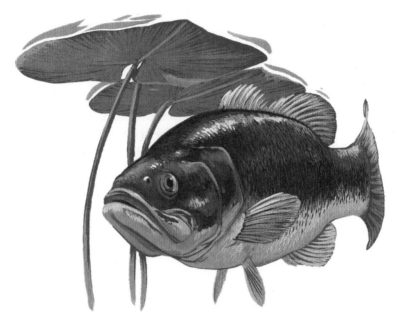

This information was just what Andrew needed, and over the next ten months, he spearheaded a fight against the housing development. He drafted petitions, wrote to state and local representatives, contacted the news media, and spoke at dozens of town meetings. Many other town residents, it turned out, also opposed the plan, and soon, Andrew had a neighborhood committee behind him.

Andrew knew, though, that people needed more housing, so he came up with an alternative to destroying the wetlands. Across town stood an abandoned drive-in movie theater. Andrew proposed that instead of destroying a precious natural area, the developer reclaim the old theater site. His concern for both nature and people paid off. After ten months, the developer withdrew his original proposal and eventually built the new neighborhood on the theater site.

As word got out about Andrew's success, local, national, and international leaders invited him to speak about environmental awareness. He traveled to the United Nations on World Earth Day in 1990 and, later, flew to Russia. Shy and reserved, Andrew initially dreaded speaking in front of other people. But with practice—and coaching from his parents—it became second nature.

Andrew's fight taught him about working with the local government, solving differences with opponents, and joining forces with others who care about protecting the environment. He urges other young people not to be afraid to take on causes they believe in—even if no one else seems interested. "Don't wait for others to become involved in environmental issues," he said. "Start protecting natural resources yourself, and others will join you."

COUNTING
EVERY TREE

Fourteen-year-old Peter Klausch marched into the mayor's office in his hometown of Welzow, Germany. He'd come, Peter told the mayor, because he was upset by the loss of trees in and around Welzow. The trees had been dying because of nearby coal mining operations and because townspeople cut down the trees for firewood and road-building projects. Peter had written to the mayor several times about the problem, but had received no response. That's why he had decided to visit the mayor in person.

After listening to Peter, the mayor raised his hands and said, "The people don't cut trees."

Peter didn't want to disagree with a public official, but he felt he had no choice. "Only last week," he told the mayor, "there were five large trees next to the road very close to here. Today they are gone."

"There never were any trees there," the mayor replied.

Peter felt angry and confused. He had always believed that public officials were supposed to look out for the community. Yet, the mayor was basically calling Peter a liar and telling him to go away. The mayor's attitude left Peter speechless, and he walked out of the mayor's office not knowing what to do. The one thing he did know was that this was not the last the mayor would hear from Peter Klausch.

By the age of fourteen, Peter already felt passionately about trees and the environment. As a youngster, his parents had taken him bicycle riding and walking through the towns and forests of

Welzow. At that time, Welzow was located in the German Democratic Republic (GDR), also known as East Germany. Peter loved to explore the villages and farms surrounding Welzow, and he felt a special connection to the oak, beech, maple, and fir forests. In the spring, the forests burst with activity as birds and other creatures hunted and foraged to feed their young. In the summer, the trees offered cool shade for resting and relaxation. The crisp chill of autumn brought mountains of leaves to dive into, and in the winter, the trees stood like silent sentinels, protecting the land and peace of the German countryside.

As he'd grown older, however, Peter became increasingly aware of the damage people were doing to the Earth. He learned about environmental problems from television documentaries and books about nature. He also observed firsthand what was happening right around his town.

Below ground in the Welzow region lay enormous deposits of brown coal, burned mainly for heat and electricity. To mine the coal, huge machines scraped off the top layers of land and then dug out the coal deposits. These hungry machines turned vast tracts of beautiful German forests into wastelands and devoured entire towns and villages.

"Around my hometown," Peter thought, "we are surrounded by a wilderness of sand and dirt from the mining, and yet these people are felling the last trees in our local environment." Peter knew he couldn't stop the coal mining, but he had to try to protect his town's own trees.

But that wasn't the only problem the mining caused. Dust from the mines smothered the surrounding woodlands, killing many of the trees. Smoke from coal burning led to horrible air pollution. This, together with the dust, contributed to asthma, lung cancer, and other illnesses among the townspeople. The air pollution also caused acid rain, which further weakened trees and poisoned lakes and streams.

Peter also noticed, however, that people were removing and damaging the trees that grew right in Welzow. "Around my home-town," Peter thought, "we are surrounded by a wilderness of sand and dirt from the mining, and yet these people are felling the last trees in our local environment." Peter knew he couldn't stop the coal mining, but he had to try to protect his town's own trees.

After his meeting with the mayor, Peter thought of an idea that might help. Earlier, he had read a book about the trees in the nearby town of Görlitz. The book had included a complete survey of the trees in Görlitz. It occurred to Peter that a survey would not only help people appreciate the trees that grew in Welzow, but would also provide him with a valuable tool to stop their destruction.

Now fifteen, Peter began his survey by locating and counting all of the trees along the road where he lived. For each tree, he recorded its height, type or species, age, and general state of health. He then counted trees along the other roads of his town. As he worked, he took time to talk to as many people as possible about the trees and the reasons why they had been damaged or removed.

"I learned a lot from the people in town," Peter said. "How they were thinking and what problems they had with trees. For instance, some people hated cleaning up the leaves in autumn and would have been happy if all the trees were cut down. Other people were nervous on windy days, because they feared that a tree could fall and damage their buildings. It was important for me to know these thoughts, because then I could work to find answers to people's problems and fears about trees. Most times, I could find compromises that would satisfy the people and save the trees."

When Peter had finished his survey, he wrote a summary of his findings. He listed all the trees in town, noting which streets still had the most trees. He also recorded his observations about how many more trees could be planted and which kinds of trees seemed to grow best in the town environment. Finally, he addressed how existing trees could be saved without causing hardships for the townspeople.

Peter delivered his report to the mayor's office, but he didn't stop there. He also wanted to protect the surrounding environment, so he extended his survey into nearby parks and woodlands.

> After reading Peter's report, the mayor could no longer deny that the town was losing trees. The city government passed new laws, making it illegal for anyone to cut down the city trees.

During this survey, he paid special attention to rare trees and shrubs. In one park, he recorded the presence of salamanders, bats, and other wildlife to point out how valuable these different places were to animals.

Peter spent almost four years completing his work. Not all of that time was pleasant. Most boys his age played soccer and rode their motorcycles through the woods. They didn't understand Peter's passion for the environment or why he spent his time doing the survey. Peter made few friends and spent most of his time working by himself. Peter's parents and several of his teachers, though, realized the importance of what he was doing. Their support and encouragement gave him the strength to continue.

When Peter had finished the second part of his survey, he again wrote up his results in a report. This time, he presented his findings not only to the mayor and city council, but to the Office of Environmental Protection, the parks commissioners, and the local mining company. To his surprise, the report attracted a great deal of interest. Both the forestry administration and the mining company called Peter and asked to meet with him. Peter used these meetings to explain how forestry and mining officials could improve the environment without spending a lot of money.

These discussions helped lead to significant improvements in the mining company practices. Now, after removing the coal from an area, the mining company carefully replaces the soil to create biotopes for plants and animals to re-establish themselves. The company also plants trees around their operations to help contain the dust from the open pits. And the Office of Environmental Protection began using Peter's report as a planning and design tool throughout eastern Germany.

Most satisfying to Peter, however, was how his work helped protect the trees in his hometown of Welzow. After reading Peter's report, the mayor could no longer deny that the town was losing trees. The city government passed new laws, making it illegal for anyone to cut down the city trees. If they do, they must plant three new trees for every young tree that is cut down and twenty-three new trees for every old tree.

Since then, other positive changes have swept through Europe. After the fall of the Berlin Wall in 1989, East and West Germany reunited into one nation. New government and private agencies were put into place, and Germans have made greater efforts to protect their environment. Burning brown coal in private homes has decreased and been replaced with cleaner-burning natural gas. Mining still takes place around Welzow, and a new coal-burning power plant has been completed, but Peter realizes that there are pressures to continue these kinds of activities.

"On the one hand," he said, "I have to understand the fact that every human uses energy—including myself. On the other hand, it is incomprehensible what people are willing to sacrifice to generate energy. So the first thing I ask myself is what each of us can do to reduce our energy use and motivate others to do the same. I also ask how in the long-term we can meet our needs without destroying so much of our planet."

Since completing his report, Peter has maintained his interest in the environment. He became involved in other environmental projects throughout Europe, teaming up with students from Denmark and Switzerland. At the Technical University in Cottbus, he completed an environmental studies program and, afterward, obtained a job working on environmental issues for a large waste recycling and disposal company. In his job, he develops strategies for reforesting waste dump sites. He also explores alternative sources of energy so people won't have to continue destroying the Earth in their search for coal.

About once a year, Peter returns to his hometown of Welzow to update his original survey of the town's trees—all 1,900 of them. Peter would like to take on other projects, but between his job and other activities, he has to be realistic. "There certainly are still points here and there about which I would like to do more," he said. "But one cannot deal with everything with one strike." For the rest of us, though, Peter's persistence and passion show how large results can grow from small ideas, and that the most important thing is simply to begin.

THE GREAT GREEN MARCH

On March 19, 1992, a paper mill discharged thousands of gallons of poisonous chemicals into the Ebro River in northeastern Spain. Authorities ordered the 15,000 people living below the mill to stop drinking water from their faucets or giving the water to their animals. People could not even use the water to bathe or wash their clothes.

The toxic spill took a huge toll on the local wildlife. Fish in the river died by the thousands. Their bodies floated downstream past dozens of small farming towns, including the village of Pina de Ebro. There, two thirteen-year-olds, Judith Pérez and Miriam Burgués Flórez, watched the dead fish float by. To them, the Ebro itself seemed to be dying.

Judith and Miriam loved the tranquil, ambling Ebro and knew it well. Each Friday, they had been going with their seventh grade nature studies class to one of the last remaining woods on the banks of the river. There, they cleaned up rubbish and learned about local flowers, birds, and reptiles from their science teacher, Javier Blasco. Now, pollution threatened the fragile ecosystem that the children cared so much about. What could they do?

The girls remembered that a week earlier, the newspapers and television stations had carried stories about a protest march by miners. "Why not have a march for the Ebro?" they asked themselves.

Judith and Miriam presented their idea to their nature studies class. They worried that people wouldn't approve, but to the

21

girls' delight, all ninety-five of their fellow students and teachers enthusiastically welcomed the idea. "From then on," one sixth-grader later wrote, "the school became a workshop, and every student, an artist. Placards, posters, rhymes, and slogans covered the desks and passages of the school. It was stupendous!"

Proudly carrying banners that read "Let's Save the Ebro" and "Water is Life," the students of Pina de Ebro School began their march on the following Tuesday. On the first day, they walked twelve kilometers (seven-and-a-half miles) to the town of La Cartuja, where they joined with students from another school and camped out. The next morning, the entire group—130 of them—walked the last eight kilometers (five miles) to Zaragoza.

As they entered the town, hundreds of other students, teachers, and parents joined the procession. The citizens of Zaragoza stared in amazement. Never before had they seen so many people express concern for the environment. Newspaper reporters showed up to cover the demonstration, dubbing it "The Great Green March" and "The Children's Walk."

But the children weren't finished yet.

In Zaragoza, Judith, Miriam, and four other youngsters met with Antonio Aragón, President of the Hydrographic Confederation. Señor Aragón was responsible for water quality and regulating the flow of water from dams farther up the river. The children handed him a written manifesto, which read:

> *The Ebro is dying. Its waters are black, it smells bad, and on its banks are fewer trees and birds and more garbage and rubbish. We want the right to enjoy the Ebro as did our grandparents. We know that with the effort of all, the Ebro will become a living river, but if there is no political will to care for it, it will be necessary to change the politicians.*

After meeting with Señor Aragon, the children met with Señor Eiroa, the president of the regional government. These meetings and the publicity the children attracted convinced local officials to begin cleaning up the Ebro. A lawsuit filed by local citizens against the polluting paper mill also led to positive changes.

Late in April, Señor Eiroa visited the town of Pina de Ebro and awarded the school with the St. George Medal of Social Merit. Judith and Miriam were pleased with the recognition and the results of their march.

"We made good friends in La Cartuja," they said. "And the march is talked about throughout the country. We learned that it is possible to get the attention of the government. We also learned

The girls remembered that a week earlier, the newspapers and television stations had carried stories about a protest march by miners. "Why not have a march for the Ebro?" they asked themselves.

23

the power of the media and the importance of being united when taking action."

Miriam and Judith know that their country has a long way to go in its efforts to protect the environment. In Spain, as in many other nations, day-to-day survival often takes priority over environmental protection. Their efforts, however, raised environmental awareness throughout Spain and planted the seeds for additional action for nature.

ON THE WING IN
AFRICA

As recently as ten years ago, the words "environment,"
"recycling," and "waste" were rarely heard in the east African country of Kenya. But today, many Kenyans—especially young people—eagerly pitch in to recycle waste, protect the environment,
and improve the daily lives of their people. One of the forces
behind this change is a young man named Vincent Ogutu.

For many people, Africa conjures up visions of vast savannahs
filled with lions and wildebeests, or mysterious rain forests inhabited by gorillas, chimpanzees, and tropical birds. African people,
we imagine, live in small villages of thatched huts far from cities
and the problems of the modern world.

In much of today's Africa, however, life couldn't be more
different.

For more and more Africans, coming face-to-face with a wild
elephant would be just as unlikely as a New Yorker running into
a grizzly bear. Day-to-day life is not filled with lions and chimpanzees, but sprawling cities, deafening traffic, and the continu-
ous struggle to survive. Over the past four decades, Africans, like
people throughout the world, have flocked to large cities by the
millions. Kenya's capital of Nairobi, for instance, now bursts with
1.5 million people—still small compared to Cairo or Lagos, but a
far cry from small-town life.

Within Nairobi's bustling metropolis lives the family of
Vincent Ogutu. Vincent was born on the outskirts of Nairobi,
in the sprawling shantytown of Mathare, an impoverished slum

where houses are made of sheet metal, mud, and scraps of wood. In Mathare, hundreds of people shared the same bathrooms, and piles of garbage filled the streets. During the rainy seasons, water pipes burst and open sewers overflowed, turning streets, yards, and alleys into rivers of mud and human waste.

Despite the poor living conditions, Vincent's parents had come to the city because it offered things they couldn't find in the countryside: schools, electricity, hospitals, and most important, jobs. In Nairobi, Vincent's father found employment as an electrician, while his mother worked making sweaters, bedsheets, and tablecloths. And despite their poverty, Vincent and his five brothers shared a happy childhood.

"In Mathare," Vincent explained, "the people were very friendly and regarded the neighbors as part of a larger family.

> Walking early in the morning with his parents or cousins, Vincent often stepped in tracks left by prowling leopards. In nearby Lake Victoria, he heard the bellows of hippos and watched crocodiles slip silently into the water.

I enjoyed my early childhood, playing with my friends in muddy water, making models of cars using mud, and playing hide-and-seek."

For his first seven years of life, Vincent didn't know any other life outside of Kenya's noisy capital. But then, a new world suddenly opened before him. One summer, Vincent's parents took him and his brothers to their home village in Nyanza Province, about 500 kilometers (300 miles) from Nairobi. This is where Vincent's parents grew up, and here, Vincent discovered a part of his family—and himself—that he'd never known.

Most Kenyans are part of a complex weave of family and clan relationships. Vincent's parents were part of the Karuoth Clan, which was, in turn, part of a larger community called the Koreyo Family. This community was spread across an area of about ten square kilometers (four square miles) in Nyanza Province.

In his parents' village, Vincent met many of his relatives for the first time and, just as important, came into contact with Africa's natural environment. The village lay nestled in a hilly region full of baboons, monkeys, hyenas, and antelope. Walking early in the morning with his parents or cousins, Vincent often stepped in tracks left by prowling leopards. In nearby Lake Victoria, he heard the bellows of hippos and watched crocodiles slip silently into the water.

More than any other animals, though, it was the birds that caught Vincent's attention. Every morning, he would watch hadada ibises flying south, making loud croaking sounds as they flew to feeding areas. In the evening, he watched the birds flapping home. Vincent asked his relatives who was directing the birds and where they were going. His relatives often shooed him away for asking such "silly" questions or gave him answers such as, "They fly north to say their prayers at night." But Vincent remained curious.

Once, he stood for almost an hour under a huge blue gum tree filled with over 200 birds called spekes weavers. As Vincent watched, these amazing creatures wove delicate nests from blades of grass, patiently stitching them together, one by one.

As Vincent learned to identify local birds, his parents told him that his clan shared a special relationship with these winged creatures. "Our clan founder was Jack Owiny," Vincent explained. "And the name Owiny means birds. Owiny saved our clan—the Karuoth Clan—from hunger and thirst by allowing a dove to show him the way through times of hardship. Today, we don't eat doves or pigeons as a tribute to our clan founder."

Unfortunately, Vincent's month-long vacation in the country passed all too quickly. Soon, he and his family boarded the bus for the eight-hour ride back to Nairobi. But Vincent carried with him something that would profoundly change his life: a passionate love for wildlife—especially birds.

Upon his return, Vincent joined the Wildlife Clubs of Kenya. His school also began organizing field trips to Kenya's world-famous national parks, nature preserves, and bird sanctuaries. Vincent always eagerly participated. As his knowledge increased, his desire to share his experiences and his love of nature also grew.

At Jamhuri High School, Vincent joined the school's wildlife club and directed his energy toward projects to benefit wild animals and the Nairobi environment. He set up bird-feeding stations, started a fish pond, and organized regular clean-ups of the

school grounds. But Vincent especially enjoyed getting kids and young adults out of the city and showing them the natural homes they all shared.

For one of his first trips, he arranged an expedition for poor, local students to Stave National Park. Vincent and the other students piled into a large truck and rode through the breathtaking park observing buffalo, giraffes, and antelope. After a few hours, the group encountered a male lion standing just off the road. The driver stopped, and the kids began taking pictures when, suddenly, the lion roared and rushed toward the truck.

In a panic, the kids dove under seats and threw themselves flat on the floor. To make matters worse, the truck stalled, and the driver couldn't get it started again. They didn't have a gun, and the lion was bellowing only a few feet away. No one dared to get out and push the truck. The group didn't have a radio, either, so they couldn't call for help. Finally, the driver realized they were on a slope and put the truck into neutral. As the truck coasted down the hill, he was able to restart the engine and return the children to park headquarters—safely and with a great story to tell.

Inspired by adventures like these, Vincent organized dozens of other trips for people from all backgrounds, from the very poor to the middle class. In the national parks, Vincent introduced the young people to lions, elephants, giraffes, zebras, and many other animals. He explained how the animals lived and how both animals and people depend on their environments to survive. Vincent took special pleasure in sharing his love of birds, and his efforts changed some of the children's lives.

"Many of the children had never before been outside of the city," Vincent explained. "They really enjoyed the trips, and most looked forward to participating more and more. Some began working harder in school so they could become botanists, tour guides, and veterinary surgeons, as well as conservationists. The majority learned to identify all of the animals and birds they saw."

After he graduated from high school in 1991, Vincent continued to organize trips for Nairobi's youth. As a member of the Nairobi National Museums Ornithology Department, Vincent visited forests, deserts, wetlands, and swamps, identifying birds and sharing his knowledge with other people. Whenever he returned home, however, Vincent was shocked by the difference between Kenya's wild areas and the squalor of Nairobi's shanty-towns. He knew it was time to take action.

At his local church, Vincent established a nursery for raising indigenous trees. As shantytowns had spread out from the heart of Nairobi, most of the trees had been destroyed. But Vincent realized that, in addition to helping wildlife, trees created a bet-ter environment for people. Over the next few years, he led other young people in raising and planting hundreds of native trees in and around his neighborhood.

Another huge problem was trash. "Garbage collection was practically nonexistent within the city limits," Vincent explained. "So I organized bimonthly clean-ups. I started with a simple waste management project within the church. Other youths and I col-lected waste paper for recycling, as well as tin cans and bottles. We also collected food and garden wastes so that we could com-post them and sell them to florists as mulch." Vincent set up a dem-onstration center where people could learn how to start similar projects in their own neighborhoods.

It wasn't long before Vincent's hard work, energy, and activ-ism attracted attention. In November 1993, the Ministry of Cultural and Social Services chose Vincent to represent Kenya at a meet-ing for the Commonwealth Youth Program in Namibia. There, he served on a committee that dealt with the environment, health, unemployment, and other issues affecting young people. The youths lobbied for national policies to be implemented across Africa. These included provisions for food security, environmen-tal protection, and an end to war.

Since then, Vincent has continued to work for the environ-ment and learn about nature. He earned a bachelor's of science degree in chemistry and would like to become an environmental chemist so he can work on waste management in his country. Meanwhile, he works as a medical representative for a pharma-ceutical company and continues to introduce young people to

Kenya's amazing wildlife. Many other young people have joined him in improving urban areas and protecting the environment.

"In Kenya, there are now many success stories of young people involving themselves with environmental cleanup and recycling," Vincent explained. "The Uvumbuzi youth group makes fertilizer from biodegradables and sells it to support their activities. The Mathare Youth Sports Club cleans up neighborhoods and plants trees and flowers in an effort to beautify the areas."

Problems remain, including pollution, overpopulation, and lack of education, but Vincent takes great satisfaction in what he and others have accomplished. Together, he and other young people are working hard to help lead Kenya—and all of Africa—toward a brighter future.

THE FORGOTTEN SIDE
OF WAR

Nadia al-Gosaibi felt nervous and awkward when her mother dropped her off at the Wildlife Rescue Center. At age thirteen, she knew she wasn't supposed to work at the center, since volunteers were supposed to be at least sixteen years old. In fact, as soon as she walked through the door, she noticed that she was the youngest person in sight.

But before Nadia could change her mind, one of her mother's friends hurried up to her and asked, "Are you ready to work?" Within minutes, Nadia found herself fetching supplies, running errands, and opening boxes as other volunteers placed struggling cormorants, grebes, and other seabirds into the boxes for safekeeping.

Nadia lived in Jubail, Saudi Arabia, only a few miles from the Kuwait border. At that time, hundreds of thousands of American, British, and other foreign soldiers were arriving in northern Saudi Arabia, turning Nadia's home into a giant staging area for the war with Iraq. But as dozens of countries fought to force back Iraqi troops and liberate Kuwait, they overlooked one important casualty of the conflict: the Arabian Gulf's wildlife.

During the war to liberate Kuwait, many of the pipelines that carried crude oil from Kuwait's oil fields to tankers in the Arabian Gulf were bombed. The ruptured pipelines spilled millions of barrels of thick, raw petroleum into the gulf, coating the sea surface for hundreds of square miles and drifting south along the

coast of Saudi Arabia. The oil killed fish, coastal mangrove trees, coral reefs, sea turtles, and thousands of sea birds.

In the wake of this environmental disaster, officials from Saudi Arabia's National Commission for Wildlife Conservation and Development launched a major effort to save the wildlife, especially birds. They set up the rescue center in Jubail, and dozens of volunteers came from all over the world to help. Many off-duty soldiers also volunteered at the center. Around the same time, the government temporarily closed all schools in Jubail, including Nadia's. A friend of Nadia's mother suggested that the center could use a pair of extra hands.

"At first, I worked at very simple tasks," Nadia recalled. "I opened boxes for the birds to be put in and then shut them quickly so the birds couldn't get out." Soon, she was feeding birds

Within minutes, Nadia found herself fetching supplies, running errands, and opening boxes as other volunteers placed struggling cormorants, grebes, and other seabirds into the boxes for safekeeping.

and checking them for broken bones and other injuries. Then, other volunteers taught her how to administer first aid to injured animals and how to perform the difficult task of cleaning oil-soaked birds.

Cleaning a single bird took about two hours. Two volunteers worked as a team, one holding the bird still, the other carefully washing each individual feather of the bird. Usually, the bird would need to be washed several times before the last of the oil had dissolved. After a thorough rinsing, it joined other birds in a special recovery area at the center.

Nadia learned her tasks quickly and soon knew enough to teach other volunteers. She met people from Saudi Arabia, Britain, the United States, the Netherlands, and Japan, and often acted as an interpreter, translating from English to Arabic and back again. During her three months at the center, she helped process hundreds of birds. Many died, but fortunately, others recovered and were released in safe areas far away from the hostilities.

Afterward, Nadia returned to school and gradually resumed her normal life. Eventually, she went to college and is now studying in England to be an aerospace manufacturing engineer. Her experiences working at the center, however, remain fresh in her memory. She fondly remembers the other volunteers at the center and takes a lasting satisfaction in the work that she did there.

"Every bird in this world should have the right to be free and healthy," she said. "The work I did was the least I could do to give them this right. And now, every time I walk along the coast and see a cormorant or grebe, I wonder if it could be one of the birds I helped return to freedom."

PROTECTING AN
ANCIENT WOODLAND

Early one morning, before school, thirteen-year-old Alice Hyde rubbed her eyes, pulled on her purple jacket, and wrapped a red wool scarf around her neck. "Come on Ben!" she called. Her family's floppy-eared golden retriever rushed at her from the living room, his tail wagging excitedly. Alice patted her dog on the head and snapped the leash on Ben's jiggling collar. "I'll be back in a little while," she yelled to her mom. Then, she and Ben bounded out the door.

Ben towed Alice along their neighborhood sidewalks for several blocks. The streets had already awakened by now, with commuters cranking up their automobiles and the roar of outer London filling the chilly morning air. Five minutes later, Alice and Ben crossed one last street and stepped into a world as tranquil as London was agitated. It was Alice's favorite place, Oxleas Wood.

Following the dirt path into the 130-hectare (321-acre) park never failed to make Alice feel more alive. Spirit-like mist rose from the damp, leaf-covered ground and wafted mysteriously through the ancient oaks reaching overhead. Moss covered the four-foot wide tree trunks, conjuring up images of Robin Hood and his Merry Band in Alice's mind.

Oxleas Wood, though, had been around long before Robin Hood. Over 8,000 years old, the forest had survived storms, droughts, and human activities since the last ice age. Even during the twentieth century, as London's rapid development devoured open space in all directions, this peaceful nature area had been

"When I got that letter, I was really angry," Alice said. "...So I decided to have a children's demonstration."

spared the axe and bulldozer. In 1936, the old county council had acquired the forest to hold in perpetuity for the enjoyment and use of all Londoners. Now, it was one of only three ancient forest fragments that survived in the greater London area.

Living only minutes away, Alice was able to enjoy the wood more than most. Walking Ben among the majestic trees every morning, Alice thrilled at the birds, insects, and other wildlife she spotted all around her. Kicking up autumn leaves, Alice treasured the forest for giving her a place to think and clear her head before a busy day of school and chores.

When Alice returned home on this particular morning, however, unwelcome news awaited her. Her parents sat at their kitchen table, finishing their breakfast tea with the London *Times* spread out in front of them. Looking up from the paper, her father said, "Looks like they're going to go ahead with the highway through Oxleas Wood after all."

"What?" Alice cried.

Alice had heard about a plan by the Department of Transport to build a four-lane highway through Oxleas. The new road would connect the London Docklands—an industrial area across the river—to a highway. The Greenwich Council, together with a group known as the Oxleas Nine, had been fighting the road, but Alice had been so busy with school that she hadn't paid much attention. Suddenly, though, she felt as if thousands of automobiles were roaring toward her, trying to run down her family, her neighborhood, and her favorite place.

"I knew I had to do something," Alice said.

That afternoon, after school, she began her campaign to save Oxleas Wood. She started by writing letters to her representatives and other politicians. She explained the historic importance of the wood and its role in protecting fifty-five kinds of birds and 100 species of butterflies, as well as bats, badgers, and countless other animals. Alice also explained how important the wood was to her personally and to many other people as a refuge from the hectic metropolis surrounding them. But her pleas fell on deaf ears. She received only a few polite letters in return, including one from the Department of Transport.

"When I got that letter, I was really angry," Alice said. "They said we needed the road, but that it would be built on the east side of the wood and wouldn't destroy much wildlife....So I decided to have a children's demonstration."

Alice knew that other children also cared about Oxleas Wood and the environment, so she wrote to eighty local schools and asked children to sign a petition opposing the road. The petition proclaimed:

We, the young people of Greenwich, Lewisham, and Bexleyheath, cannot understand why the Ministry of Transport wants to put a four-lane highway through the last significant fragment of ancient woodlands in London.

If the proposed road goes ahead, Oxleas Wood will be ruined, wildlife and vegetation will be lost forever, and locals will suffer neverending noise and air pollution.

The government was distressed at the destruction of many trees due to the October 1987 hurricane. The government now intends to become a destructor of woodlands itself.

We, the future generation, demand that the government preserve Oxleas Wood for us.

Alice also sent the petition to schools outside her area, as well as colleges, universities, and other conservationists throughout England. Within a year, she had collected over 10,000 signatures. The response delighted her. She contacted local newspapers and television stations and announced that she and her fellow activists would deliver their petition and signatures to 10 Downing Street, the home of British Prime Minister John Major.

Over 150 children joined in the delivery, accompanied by noted environmentalist David Bellamy. Chanting and waving placards that stated "No East London River Crossing" and "32,000 Seasons in Oxleas Wood," they delivered their petition to a representative of the prime minister. Alice also answered questions from reporters and met with her local representative from the House of Parliament. But despite newspaper headlines that shouted "Defiant Alice tackles Major" and "Battling Alice goes to No. 10," the prime minister shrugged off the demonstration. Through his representative, he referred Alice to the minister of transport, who insisted that the road would go through one way or another.

At this point, many people would have given up, but Alice sensed a wave of opposition rising against the project. In addition to local protests, the European Commission of the European Union (EU) notified the British Government that it had not conducted a proper environmental assessment of its plan for the new highway. This violated the international treaty that bound European countries together in the EU. Newspapers and television stations ran numerous stories about the road and protests—almost all of the reports against the plan. Alice was quick to recognize the tremendous influence of this media attention. "A little more publicity," she thought, "might turn the tide against the highway. But what would make a dramatic statement?"

As she pondered her next move, Alice suddenly remembered a television commercial in which a crowd held up large signs or "flash cards." Each person had held up one piece of paper that contained only a fragment of a word or color, but together they formed dramatic messages and pictures. "I'll bet I could do that for Oxleas Wood," Alice told herself.

She immediately set out recruiting fellow students for the project. "Other kids thought I was a bit strange," she said. "But many of my friends were very supportive and pitched in." She also recruited an expert signmaker and teacher from the nearby college of art. Together, they painted their display on eighty squares cut from cardboard packing boxes.

One problem remained: How would the sign be viewed? Similar signs were always photographed from a blimp, helicopter, or tower. So Alice wrote to Richard Branson, the owner of Virgin Airways. Alice knew that Mr. Branson—an avid balloonist—owned several hot air balloons, and she asked him to provide one to fly members of the press and government over her display. He agreed.

Before the big day, Alice worried about the unpredictable English weather. "What if it rains?" she asked her mum. "What if we get fogged in and no one can see the sign?" The day of the event, however, dawned bright and clear. An excited buzz filled the air as hundreds of children, reporters, and politicians arrived at the site where the proposed road would slash into Oxleas

> Alice, the Oxleas Nine, and other opponents of the road felt optimistic that this would at last make the government realize their mistake in building the road.
>
> It didn't.

Wood. As promised, the majestic hot air balloon stood anchored and ready, and it soon carried photographers and politicians into the sky.

Under Alice's direction, eighty children, surrounded by dozens of other protestors, hoisted their sign aloft. "Save Oxleas Wood!" it proclaimed on one side. Then, flipping the sign over, the children displayed a beautiful mural of a green woodland.

The dramatic images did their job. Newspapers and television stations all over England ran photos of the sign and protest. Alice, the Oxleas Nine, and other opponents of the road felt optimistic that this would at last make the government realize their mistake in building the road.

It didn't.

Despite the protests, the government insisted that the road would be built. Alice began to feel like she was running out of options—and time—to save her favorite place.

Then, fate stepped in. One afternoon, Alice was sitting at home, staring at her latest school assignment and trying not to worry about Oxleas Wood, when the phone rang. She picked it up and found herself talking to the producer of *Blue Peter*, a children's environmental television program. The producer had been following Alice's battle to save Oxleas Wood and was impressed with her cause and dedication. The producer invited Alice to be a guest reporter on *Blue Peter* and interview people about the Oxleas Wood project. *Blue Peter* helped Alice arrange an interview with Minister of Transport Peter Norris, the man in charge of the ill-conceived road project.

With the help of her parents and friends, Alice carefully prepared questions to ask the minister and her other guests. She planned to firmly question the minister about the road and felt confident she could sway television viewers in favor of protecting Oxleas.

At the last minute, however, Mr. Norris called and pulled out of the interview. Alice felt devastated, but she continued on with the show. On *Blue Peter,* she spent five minutes explaining the road scheme and the destruction it would inflict on Oxleas Wood. She also interviewed dozens of children and adults, asking them how they felt about the road. All except one were dead-set against the project. When the program was broadcast, their messages reached hundreds of thousands of people all over London. One of those people just happened to be Mr. Norris's seven-year-old son, Edward.

"My son rang me up immediately after the program," Mr. Norris later explained, "and asked me what I was going to do about Oxleas. I was obliged to give him a very detailed technical reply of the choices available." Edward wasn't convinced and urged his father to reconsider the road. Under pressure from his own son, as well as thousands of other protestors, the minister reluctantly agreed to reopen the investigation of the road. Now, other members of Parliament felt free to reconsider the project. In July 1993—as a national election approached—the government announced that it was putting construction of the controversial road on hold until they could conduct a thorough review. In 1997, after another national election, the Oxleas Road project was cancelled altogether.

Alice and the thousands of other people who had joined in the protests celebrated. "I'm very pleased to hear the news," Alice said. "I hope it will encourage other adults and children to get involved and stand up for what they believe in."

After the celebrations had died down, Alice resumed her normal life. She still took Ben for walks through Oxleas every morning and took extra satisfaction in knowing that the woods were out of harm's way. Schoolwork, which she had put on the back burner during the campaign, once again became the focus of her life. As she prepared to study English at Leeds University, however, her experience campaigning to save Oxleas helped her think about the world's other problems.

"Because of the campaign, I now question everything," she said. "You should not accept things at face value. You should always question it. The campaign made me more skeptical, but it also helped me develop my debating skills and see both sides of an issue." Besides helping to save a natural treasure, Alice has provided us with lessons in commitment, dedication, and perseverance—lessons we can all use as we stand up for what we believe.

EXPLORERS WITH A
DIFFERENCE

Throughout his boyhood in Mexico's Yucatán Peninsula, Elias Miguel Alcocer Puerto had read about the proud, ancient civilization of the Mayans. He'd learned of their spectacular city-states, marvelous stone pyramids, advanced scientific knowledge, and the tropical forests that were their home.

Now, Elias was taking his first journey through the ancient homelands of the Mayans. A local priest and family friend had invited Elias on the trip to tour the rural villages of the modern Mayan people. Elias himself was a descendent of the Mayans, but he'd grown up in Merida, the capital city of the Yucatán. He was eager to see for himself how more traditional Mayans lived.

Traveling from village to village, however, Elias grew more and more dismayed. Instead of a thriving civilization, he discovered people living in poverty. Many of the rich forests had been burned or cut down, and the people scratched a meager living farming the barren, worn-out soils.

Moved by the economic situation in the villages and the plight of the Yucatán's remaining forests and wildlife, Elias saved up the money he earned as a dishwasher and began heading to the countryside at every opportunity. Often traveling alone, he was invited to stay in the homes of families and made friends with many people. As his friendships grew, he learned more about the Mayans' lives and was able to better appreciate their culture.

When he was fifteen years old, Elias organized a group called Explorers of the Mayab, made up of both urban and rural youths.

Growing up, Elias had often felt ignored by adults. His major motivation in forming the Explorers was to give other young people a chance to express themselves and be heard. At first, the group simply camped and hiked together. As they got to know each other, though, the group decided to tackle their first project: a waste disposal program for one of the villages.

Many rural towns had no system for dealing with garbage. As a result, it piled up everywhere, attracting rats and flies and creating a public health hazard. In the town of Mani, the Explorers helped relieve these problems by installing trash cans and organizing a system to collect and bury wastes.

Encouraged by this success, the Explorers began looking into ways to help the farmers and save the remaining forest. They contacted agricultural agencies in the United States to learn about farming methods that protected the soil and didn't destroy

Moved by the economic situation in the villages and the plight of the Yucatán's remaining forests and wildlife, Elias saved up the money he earned as a dishwasher and began heading to the countryside at every opportunity.

the rain forest. They also learned how to plant certain crops with others to help repel insect pests.

Elias and the Explorers knew they couldn't solve everyone's problems by themselves, but they shared their information with rural farmers and found that some were eager to experiment with the new methods. Elias also sought out opportunities to expand his own knowledge and training. In 1991, he and two other "yucatecos" visited California to take part in a "Program of Exchange and Leadership in Conservation for Young People of Mexico and the United States." In this summer program, sponsored by Partners of the Americas and the Student Conservation Association, Elias learned about other approaches to working on environmental issues. Elias also helped five other Mexican youths participate in a similar conservation program in Iowa. These exchanges allowed the yucatecos to meet other youths from Mexico and the United States who were working to improve society and protect the environment.

Today, back in Mexico, Elias and the Explorers continue to learn about their world and work on projects with the Yucatán's rural people. Their greatest success, though, is motivating youths to become actively involved in their communities and helping them realize that they do have a say in their own destinies.

PENGUIN RESCUE

Ten-year-old Tom Delamore stood at the bow of the Waiheke Island ferry. With the sun warming his face and his hair fluttering in the breeze, he felt tired but good. He and the rest of his soccer team were riding home from Auckland, where they'd played a match that morning. They'd won the game, and Tom had played well. After the morning's excitement, he looked forward to a relaxing afternoon with his family. Maybe he would read the latest issue of the *Kiwi Conservation Club Newsletter* that had arrived the previous day. Or maybe, toward sunset, he would walk down to the sea wall to watch the little blue penguins return from their day of catching fish.

Penguins had played an important part in Tom's life. When he was four, Tom's parents had read him a story called "Pippa the Penguin," and Tom had become enchanted with the waddling, "tuxedoed" birds. Ever since, he'd collected penguin ornaments, plastered his room with penguin posters, and devoured books and movies about the world's seventeen or so penguin species. Unlike most children, though, Tom had real penguins living right in his backyard.

A half-dozen different kinds of penguins live in and around New Zealand. The world's smallest, the little blue penguin, lived and nested right in Tom's home, Waiheke Island. At dawn each morning, they waddled out of their burrows, located in the rocks of the sea wall near the ferry dock. Reaching the ocean, these awkward walkers transformed themselves into some of the world's fastest, sleekest swimmers. They plunged into the surf and raced far out into the gulf. Diving and surfacing, they spent the day

stuffing themselves on fish and squid. Just after sunset, they returned to shore, shook the sea water from their well-oiled feathers, and waddled back into their burrows.

Tom loved watching the penguins. Besides those living in
the sea wall, several lived under the woolshed on his family's farm.
Whenever he got a chance, Tom would slip out of the house at
dawn or sunset to watch the blue-backed birds as they comically
staggered to or from the sea. Over the years, Tom got to know the
penguins as if they were his family. He knew what they ate, when
they got up and went to bed, and when they nested and raised
their young. He felt very protective of his miniature "relatives."

As the noon ferry approached the wharf at Matiatia Bay, however, Tom's pulse suddenly raced with alarm. There, next to the
wharf, a large mechanical digger was tearing away the rocks of the
sea wall—the very place where the little blue penguins lived!

A sense of dread filled Tom. He and his family lived in one of the three houses near the wharf, and as soon as the ferry touched the dock, Tom sprinted home and burst through the front door.

"Mom!" he cried. "They're burying the penguins!"

"What?" his mom, Jude, asked, also alarmed. For weeks, she and Tom had been watching heavy equipment gather to begin construction of a new wharf. As more and more people had moved to Waiheke Island, the old wharf could no longer accommodate the increased ferry traffic. Jude, though, had assured her son that someone would be looking out for the penguins. She was wrong.

"We have to stop them," Tom told his mother.

"Come on," Jude said. "I'll go with you."

Together, they hurried to the construction site. The sound of the large diesel engine roared in Tom's ears as the digger tore at the sea wall to make way for the new wharf. Tom saw, though, that the work had not proceeded as far as he had thought. Only one penguin burrow had been damaged so far. Nonetheless, he felt a sense of urgency as he and his mother entered the construction zone.

Tom and his mother walked up to a man in an orange hard hat. Although Tom was tall for his age, the man towered over him. Tom could feel his tongue stick to the roof of his mouth. Reserved by nature, he was tempted to flee back to his house and forget the whole thing. But when he watched the giant digger take another bite out of the sea wall, Tom knew he had to take action.

"Sir?" Tom croaked, his heart thumping in his ears. "Are you the person in charge?"

The man in the orange hard hat looked down at him. "What?" he yelled over the growl of the digger.

"Are you in charge?" Tom shouted.

"Yes! What of it?"

"You've got to stop this digging now. You're burying the little blue penguins!"

The man looked at Tom and his mother as though they'd just landed from Mars. "No one told me about any penguins," he said.

> Tom's pulse suddenly raced with alarm. There, next to the wharf, a large mechanical digger was tearing away the rocks of the sea wall—the very place where the little blue penguins lived!

With the digger scraping and rasping only a few yards away, Tom explained that he'd been watching the little blue penguins come to the sea wall for years. He told the man how the penguins left during the day to feed out in the Hauraki Gulf and returned at night to sleep inside their sea wall burrows.

The foreman waved his hand impatiently. "I haven't seen any penguins," he told Tom and his mother.

Tom led the man along the rocks. "Look here," Tom said, pointing out the white fishy-smelling droppings that carpeted the entrance to each penguin burrow.

The foreman remained skeptical. "Maybe they've gone away."

Just then, a small, dark shape, a foot-and-a-half high, darted between two rocks.

"Look!" Tom shouted.

Seeing the little blue penguin for himself softened the foreman's attitude. "Well," the man admitted. "If there's one, there are probably others. I'll stop work for an hour, but hurry up. This is costing me a lot of money."

Tom and his mother knew they had to act fast. Fortunately, Tom's father worked for New Zealand's Department of Conservation (DOC). Within a short time, he arrived at the construction site with members of the local city council. Tom's father informed the foreman and city council members that the little blue penguin was a protected species and that destroying their homes was

illegal. Tom's father asked that they delay working on the new wharf until the DOC could help supervise the project. Neither the city council nor the construction company wanted to be responsible for killing the protected birds, so they reluctantly agreed to postpone the sea wall demolition until the following week.

The next Monday, Tom and his family joined a team of two DOC officers, two city council workers, and the city council manager down by the sea wall. Tom had been worried that this new team wouldn't be able to locate all of the penguin burrows, so he had spent the weekend marking each burrow entrance with bright orange spray paint. Now, with Tom's orange marks leading the way, the team proceeded to make sure each burrow was empty so that the boulders could be moved for the new wharf.

At first, the city council workers tried to look into each burrow with flashlights and reach in with their hands to locate the penguins. The deep, twisting passageways, however, proved impossible to check in this way. Then someone suggested using the digger—the same one that had been used to destroy the wall— to lift the boulders covering the burrows.

Working slowly and carefully, the digger operator exposed each burrow one by one. Every time he came up empty, and the construction crew and city council members began to doubt that the birds really used the sea wall. Tom was troubled. He knew the penguins needed these burrows, but without finding any living penguins, he'd have a hard time convincing the adults to safeguard his feathered friends.

When he heard some of the adults grumble to themselves, Tom felt close to panic. He tried to explain that the penguins were probably out feeding and that if they just waited until evening, they'd see plenty of penguins. The adults shrugged and went back to talking among themselves. "What am I going to do?" Tom asked himself.

Near the end of the day, however, the digger lifted one last large boulder, and Tom heard a shout.

"Yes!" one of the council workers yelled, peering into a burrow. "There's two!"

Working slowly and carefully, the digger operator exposed each burrow one by one. Every time he came up empty, and the construction crew and city council members began to doubt that the birds really used the sea wall.

Tom could finally breathe again. Wearing thick leather gloves, the city council workers caught the two frightened birds and placed them in special boxes. Tom cared for the penguins that night, and the next day, the DOC officers carried the birds across the bay to the Tiritiri Matangi Wildlife Sanctuary, where they were released.

Over the next few weeks, the digger team rescued twenty more penguins from the sea wall. The city council agreed to rebuild the sea wall as soon as the wharf was finished and to construct a new rock wall farther around the bay to encourage penguins to nest there. Within a year after the construction was finished, the penguins began moving into their new homes and continued their lives as if nothing had happened.

Not everyone appreciated Tom's efforts to save the penguins. Several of his classmates teased him about being a "tall poppy," or show off, which hurt Tom's feelings. But most people on Waiheke Island applauded him for what he had done. Reporters for local newspapers and the Kiwi Conservation Club— the children's conservation group to which Tom belonged— wrote about the penguins and what Tom had done to save them. Tom didn't expect this publicity, nor did he particularly want it. He had only wanted to help the animals he loved, not become a celebrity.

Still, Tom felt deeply satisfied knowing that he had helped the animals he cared so much about. His actions also brought a greater awareness of the penguins to the community on Waiheke Island. When they learned of the peril faced by the penguins, dozens of community members joined in to help catch and relocate the birds. Now, when the ferries come in from Auckland, many people linger to watch the penguins return from their day of fishing out in the Hauraki Gulf. Tom not only saved the penguins living near his home—he helped bring people and penguins closer together in the community they both share.

LANDFILL ROCK

The town of Durango, Colorado, was being buried
alive. Not by a volcano or avalanche, but by a mountain of trash.
Like many other places in the world, La Plata County—where
Durango is located—disposed of its solid waste by burying it in
landfills just outside of town. By 1991, however, one of its two
landfills was almost full, while the second had been scheduled to
close because of new, tighter regulations by the United States
Environmental Protection Agency. As space and time were running out, La Plata County looked as if it would be left holding the
bag—the garbage bag.

Faced with this crisis, county policymakers hired a consult-
ant to explore its options. Should they expand their recycling
programs to reduce waste? Open a new landfill in a heavily-used
recreational area? Truck their wastes to other counties in Colorado
and New Mexico? As the debate over what to do heated up, thirteen-year-old David Gilford knew he'd found the right topic for
his independent studies project at Smiley Middle School.

Together with four friends—Josh Bennett, Chelsi Brown,
Cody McInnes, and Bryan McCoy—David decided to make a
video about La Plata County's dump dilemma and its possible
solutions. The project appealed to David for two reasons. First,
he'd long been committed to environmental issues, in great part
because of his parents' strong beliefs in taking care of the earth.
Even before they'd been assigned a class project, he and his friends
had been looking for a way to tackle some environmental issue.
Second, David's mother was a filmmaker, and David loved using
cameras and other technical equipment. Making the video would

give him and his classmates a chance to learn more about the high-tech world while contributing to an important debate in their community.

David and his friends began by interviewing people on all sides of the debate. At first, they weren't sure people would meet with them, but almost everyone they contacted agreed to be interviewed, including the county's environmental planner, Durango's mayor, a local developer who wanted to build a new landfill, and a variety of county residents. During a local meeting, they were even able to ask the governor of Colorado a question about the issue. The young filmmakers also shot footage of two county commission meetings where the waste proposals were debated, and visited the landfill sites, where they filmed tractors burying old refrigerators, plastic bottles, and construction waste.

When they were finished, David and his friends had accumulated over twenty hours of videotape. They made arrangements to use the editing facilities at Fort Lewis College in Durango. Over the next several weeks, they cut their twenty hours of raw videotape down to a twenty minute story. "It took persistence," David recalled. "Video editing is very time-consuming, and we spent long hours logging the interviews and then piecing together short segments." After that, they dubbed in their narration and added a rock 'n' roll soundtrack. "It was much more fun than going to school," David added with a laugh.

After completing the video, however, David and his friends felt nervous about showing it. Was it any good? Would adults take it seriously?

They decided to give the video a trial run at a local Sierra Club meeting. When the video ended, the Sierra Club audience broke into cheers and applause, giving a huge boost to the students' confidence. Over the next few months, they showed the film to the Durango City Council, the mayor, and the La Plata County Commissioners. The film not only gave a balanced presentation of all sides of the landfill issue, but emphasized the benefits of recycling and composting in reducing waste, saving money, and protecting the environment.

David's video received enthusiastic response wherever it was shown. Unfortunately, even after seeing the film, La Plata County's decisionmakers chose to ignore recycling as a serious option for their waste-management woes. Instead, they decided to begin trucking waste to New Mexico, adding to the southern Colorado's air pollution and contributing to traditional dead-end waste strategies.

David and his friends, however, learned a lot from their experience. "By clearly placing recycling as an alternative to putting waste in a landfill," David explained, "I feel that our video encouraged decisionmakers to think about recycling not as simply a public service, but as an alternative to waste disposal, which has been increasing in cost over the past seven years."

> After completing the video, however, David and his friends felt nervous about showing it. Was it any good? Would adults take it seriously?

"We also showed," David added, "that we were capable of creating a coherent video that could capture the public's attention. Whether politicians did the right thing or not—and in general, they did not—was indicative not of our project's success or failure, but rather of the political system itself. Even though we felt the wrong decisions were made, they at least were made by people who knew more about the issue than before our project. *That* is progress."

One of the important things David and his friends discovered was just how poorly-informed most people—including public officials—were about waste issues. To address that situation, the young filmmakers produced public service announcements to educate people about how to properly sort their waste for recycling. They also received several awards and honors for their efforts, including the Navajo Youth Award for promoting environmental awareness.

"The project was certainly an empowering experience," David said. "Five middle-school kids were able to get the full attention of policy-making adults, both through the video and through personal interaction. I would encourage people of any age to get involved in issues that interest and concern them. The methods we used in our project apply equally well to any topic of concern. Identify key people and concepts, research and ask questions, record the results, and combine the raw material into a cohesive argument."

Meanwhile, La Plata County's landfill issue is far from over. David is now a student at Williams College and Oxford University, but some of the recycling options he and his friends promoted are still possibilities for the future. Their video and public service announcements reached fresh audiences when recently broadcast on Durango's new public access television station, keeping hope alive that La Plata County and other communities will find sensible, environmentally-sound solutions to their landfill woes.

HEALING THE DESERT

Aishah Ali Abakar Barnawi, eleven years old, sat high among the summits of the Aja' Mountains in northern Saudi Arabia. Spectacular beauty surrounded her. Granite domes and spires, sculpted by millions of years of wind and rain, stretched out in all directions. Lavender and pink rocks framed small groves of wild date palms. Overhead, griffon vultures and fan-tailed ravens circled in the desert breeze.

Aishah loved this place. In the desert, she always found something fascinating to appreciate and enjoy. But she was also growing tired. This was her tenth day in a row coming to this same spot. Each morning, she would climb up into these breathtaking mountains with a researcher from Saudi Arabia's Wildlife Commission. As dawn swept light across the sky, they'd set up their spotting telescopes. For the next twelve hours, they would wait. And wait.

She understood the importance of her work, but at times—like this day—she felt as if she would be waiting here the rest of her life. The waiting was even harder since it was the Islamic holy month of Ramadan, when Muslims do not eat or drink from dawn until sunset. Aishah's stomach rumbled like thunder. She wanted nothing more than to drink a tall, cool glass of water and eat a meat-filled sambusa pastry.

Aishah's mind grew fuzzy and her head began to nod. Suddenly, from far away, wild cries reached Aishah's ears. Her head snapped up. "Could this be them?"

Adapted from the original story by Othman Llewelyn of the National Commission for Wildlife Conservation and Development, Saudi Arabia

> Suddenly, from far away, wild cries reached Aishah's ears. Her head snapped up. "Could this be them?"

Peering through her spotting scope, Aishah scanned the skies in the direction of the noise. She didn't see them right away. After several minutes, though, she saw the magnificent birds she had been waiting for: the demoiselle cranes.

Demoiselle cranes are large birds, standing up to 100 cm (three feet) tall, with wingspans of 185 cm (over five feet). Each spring, the cranes migrate from marshes in central Sudan and Chad—the land of Aishah's Bornu ancestors—to their breeding grounds in Central Asia. On the way, they pass over the Aja' Mountains in Saudi Arabia, often stopping to rest, drink, and feed.

The problem was that no one knew how many cranes there were. Migrating birds face many dangers, both natural and manmade. During migration, birds may get lost or die from exhaustion or starvation. They can fly into power lines or get shot by hunters. In both their summer and winter homes, key feeding or nesting areas may be destroyed by human activities such as farming and pesticide use.

Though the cranes spent only a few days in Saudi Arabia, scientists at the National Commission for Wildlife Conservation and Development felt it was important to know how many cranes passed through each year. Periodic censuses would allow them to determine whether the crane population was stable, increasing, or decreasing. Aishah had volunteered to help with the very first crane census, and finally, her patience was rewarded.

With the great trumpeting birds fixed in her binoculars, Aishah began counting. In the first flock she counted forty-five cranes and quickly scribbled the number down. Soon, larger flocks followed the first. "There are too many!" Aishah told the wildlife researcher next to her.

The researcher grinned and said, "Try counting the wings and divide by two!"

"Thanks a lot," Aishah thought with a laugh. Still, she did the best she could, tallying the number of birds as they flew overhead. She also took compass bearings to determine which way the birds were headed. Over the next few days, Aishah and the other crane counters tallied 4,500 cranes. Biologists used this information to make plans for protecting the cranes and for working with wildlife conservation agencies in Africa and Central Asia. Counting cranes, though, was only one part of Aishah's efforts to protect Saudi Arabia's animals and the homes they lived in.

One of twelve children, Aishah grew up in the city of Mecca (or "Makkah" in Arabic), the holiest place in the Muslim world. It is a sanctuary where no wild animals or plants may be destroyed or injured. Mecca is the birthplace of Muhammad, the prophet whose teachings form the basis for Islam, one of the world's great religions. Here, Aishah took an interest in nature at an early age. This interest was fostered by her neighbor, who worked for Saudi Arabia's National Commission for Wildlife Conservation and Development. The neighbor worked all over Saudi Arabia and sometimes brought home animals he had rescued from people who had captured them or from other dangers.

Aishah loved to visit and learn about these animals and help return them to the wild. She especially loved reptiles and enjoyed sharing what she had learned with other children and adults in her neighborhood. Saudi Arabia is home to many venomous snakes, and many Saudi Arabians—like people elsewhere—are terrified of *all* snakes. Aishah, though, patiently talked about the animals and their importance.

Picking up a purplish-brown Arabian cat snake, she would quickly attract a crowd. "Most kinds of snakes aren't venomous," she would tell the mesmerized people around her. "This one is, but its venom is too weak and its fangs are too far back in its mouth to harm people. It uses its venom to subdue its prey— lizards, birds, and mice. Anyhow, I never hurt him, so he doesn't try to bite."

Some of her favorite reptiles were the large lizards called spiny-tailed dhabbs. "The spiny-tailed dhabbs are funny," she explained. "Sometimes they are calm, and then suddenly they get frightened for no reason at all and run away as fast as they can." To help people overcome their fears of these animals, Aishah would recite verses from the Islamic holy book, the Qur'an: "There is no animal on the earth, nor any bird that wings its flight, but is a people like yourselves."

"Nothing has been created without purpose," she added. "Treat every thing with reverence for its Creator."

When she was nine years old, Aishah and her family received a special opportunity. Their neighbor invited them to accompany him to Saudi Arabia's National Wildlife Research Center, where endangered animals were being bred for reintroduction into their native habitats. Here, for the first time, Aishah saw gazelles, oryx, bustards, ostriches, caracals, and other endangered species.

Many of the animals at the research center were kept in large enclosures where they were free to roam around, much as they would in the wild. While Aishah was hiking through one of these enclosures, she had an unforgettable encounter. She spotted several ibex grazing among the rocks and began walking slowly, but steadily, toward them. Soon, she came face-to-face with the male that dominated the herd. It stood one meter (over three feet) tall, and its horns curved back like scimitars. When it shook its skin, a fine layer of dust rose from its glossy brown coat. The ibex dwarfed Aishah with its power and size, but it made no move to harm her. Instead, the ibex and Aishah simply stared into each other's eyes.

After a minute or two, Aishah backed away from the ibex, but the large mammal left its mark on her consciousness. Workers at the wildlife center told Aishah that hunters had killed off the ibex and other wild animals from many parts of the Arabian Peninsula. Decades of overgrazing by domestic camels, sheep, and goats had also stripped the land of nutritious plants for wild animals to eat.

Aishah wanted to help restore the desert for the ibex and other wildlife. Through her neighbor, she asked the secretary general of the Wildlife Commission if she could participate in their work. Her request created quite a stir. No child had ever asked to do such work—let alone a girl! In Saudi Arabia, like some other countries, wildlife conservation is done mainly by men. To have a girl volunteer to work alongside them seemed unusual indeed. The secretary general, however, wanted to encourage Aishah's enthusiasm and sincerity, so he agreed to her request.

During vacations from school, Aishah began visiting and learning about the desert. She soon felt at home.

"I love the desert," she explained. "I love it more than the city. It is beautiful and pure. In the desert I feel peaceful and happy. The desert smells and sounds different at different seasons. Sometimes I smell acacia flowers, sometimes I smell wormwood,

and sometimes I smell dust. Sometimes I hear birds singing, and sometimes I hear only the wind."

With the help of wildlife rangers, Aishah learned how to use a compass and read a map; how to tell directions by the sun, moon, and stars; and how to recognize the tracks of different animals. Wearing clothes the color of desert sands, she learned to approach animals from downwind so that she could observe them at close range. Aishah kept a journal of the things she learned and saw. She drew pictures of plants, animals, and landscapes. She pressed plants for the national herbarium so that future scientists could refer to them, and she recorded signs of overgrazing that she encountered. Soon, Aishah also began participating in projects to help protect the desert and its inhabitants.

One of these projects was to count the demoiselle cranes. She also received an opportunity to work in the nature reserve of al-Hawtah. Al-Hawtah is a spectacular land of limestone mesas and sculpted canyons. It is also one of the places where the Wildlife Commission had been conserving ibex and would soon reintroduce gazelles back into the wild. Unfortunately, before the land could support significant numbers of ibex and gazelles, the damage caused by domestic grazing animals had to be reversed.

To help restore the land, the Wildlife Commission began constructing a series of small stone "check dams" in the dry canyons of the reserve. The dams would prevent flash floods from washing away valuable topsoil and allow plants to grow in places that had been reduced to rock and sand. The commission asked Aishah's father, an expert builder, to supervise construction of the dams.

Aishah dived into the project with enthusiasm. Working alongside her father and local children who had also volunteered to help, she gathered stones as large as she could carry and loaded them into the bed of a pickup truck. Aishah and the other children quickly filled the truck. Then, they rode atop the rock pile to where the dams were being built. Once there, they unloaded the stones and carefully arranged them to form the walls of the check dams.

> Dark clouds raced overhead, and thunder shook the desert canyons and mountains.

Aishah worked steadily, rarely pausing to rest. She worked all day and then, after a night's sleep, rose to begin working again. Finally, the dams were finished. Aishah was so exhausted that she slept all the way back to her home in Mecca, more than a thousand kilometers (600 miles) away.

One stormy day, sixteen months after building the dams, Aishah returned to al-Hawtah. Dark clouds raced overhead, and thunder shook the desert canyons and mountains. When the rain began, brown, muddy water poured over the mountain cliffs and splashed down the canyons. Instead of rushing straight out into the desert as before, the water now gathered in a series of ponds behind the check dams that Aishah had helped build. As the water seeped slowly through the check dams, it deposited its load of mud and silt in the ponds behind them. Aishah noticed that in some places, the water was flowing too swiftly through the dams. Working alone, she used small stones to quickly plug the larger holes.

The next day, the sun cast a nurturing glow over the freshly-soaked desert. Aishah measured and recorded the depth of silt and mud behind each check dam and saw with satisfaction that the dams were doing their job. "In a few more years," she said, "enough soil will gather to form a terrace of soil behind each dam. The soil will hold water so plants and even trees can grow, and the ibex and gazelles will feed on them."

With each season, these changes continue to take place. More grasses and plants—such as desert chamomile, blepharis, and asphodel—establish themselves behind the check dams. Over 300 ibex and 200 gazelles now live in the reserve. As the plants and animals have grown, so too has Aishah. Now twenty years old, she is married and raising a child of her own—her daughter, Hanaan, whose name means "compassion." Having recently completed secondary school, Aishah plans to attend the university and would like to teach.

"Most people my age are only interested in their families and shopping and television," she said. "I have met a few people my age who care about the environment, but not very many. Some people are afraid of wild animals and kill them. They haven't been to wild places, and they don't understand animals. That is why I want to teach them about wildlife."

Meanwhile, she continues to visit the desert with her husband, who works for the Wildlife Commission, and Hanaan. They camp together in the nature preserves and explore other places where they hope to set up more preserves to protect the biological diversity of Arabia. In doing so, Aishah shares with her daughter her own love of the desert and helps create a lasting legacy of caring for wildlife and restoring the earth.

HEDGEHOG HERO

Paul Chamberlain didn't find hedgehogs. They seemed to find him.

Paul grew up in Bowden, a tiny village of 250 people in the southern part of Scotland. Although humans had inhabited the region for a long time, most of the hilly landscape remained wild and wooded. People often encountered wild animals, and Paul was no exception.

One day, when he was nine years old, Paul was playing in the town park when he spotted a hedgehog on the grass. The hedgehog was about twenty centimeters (eight inches) long and, like all hedgehogs, was covered with soft fur and thousands of spines that it used for protection. Paul had always enjoyed watching hedgehogs waddle around and, when threatened, raise their spines to defend themselves. Seeing the hedgehog in the park, though, Paul realized that something was wrong. Hedgehogs are usually nocturnal creatures—they only become active at night, when they come out to eat beetles, earthworms, and earwigs. To see one out on a hot summer day spelled trouble.

Paul gently scooped up the little pincushion and carried it home. "I didn't know much about hedgehogs at that time," Paul recalled. "So I put him in a box in the shed to try and get him back to being nocturnal. A couple of days later, I realized that 'Hedgie,' as I now called him, was not very active. Luckily, there was a hedgehog expert who worked nearby, and he told me what to do."

The hedgehog, it turned out, was suffering from hypothermia. Its body temperature had cooled to dangerously low levels. After talking with the expert, Paul rushed out to the barn and

brought Hedgie inside. Paul set Hedgie's box near the fire guard, and much to Paul's relief, Hedgie soon began stirring. Paul nursed Hedgie back to health on a mixture of goats' milk and cod liver oil. After several months, Paul was able to release Hedgie back into the wild.

Hedgie was the first of many animals Paul took under his care. After Hedgie, Paul decided to learn more about wild animals and how to take care of them. Soon, people began bringing squirrels, birds, and—of course—hedgehogs to Paul. Some of the animals had been struck by cars, others suffered from disease or malnutrition. One baby hedgehog had been abandoned by its mother. Paul patiently fed the baby with an eyedropper and, later on, put it on a diet of puppy food. Paul cared for it over the winter, then released it into the wild in the spring.

Paul doesn't always know how to take care of an animal, so he often consults with the local veterinarian or with wildlife organizations. And he isn't always successful. Some injured animals have to be put to sleep, but Paul has saved dozens of others.

Besides caring for wildlife, Paul is a dedicated accordion player. He recently played in concert with a Russian virtuoso in Blackpool, England, and was invited to a competition in St. Petersburg, Russia. Now seventeen years old, he hopes to study music at London's Royal Academy of Music.

Still, Paul finds tremendous satisfaction in caring for animals. "When an animal passes through my hands successfully," he said, "I always feel good and hope that the animal will live a long life." That in itself is reward enough for him.

SEA TURTLE SEARCH

As dawn cast a rose-colored glow across the sandy beach, fourteen-year-old Christian Miller felt a sense of victory at having once again dragged himself out of bed. Though it was hard to get up so early day after day, he always felt more alive early in the morning. He relished breathing in the fresh, salty air off the Atlantic Ocean and appreciated the last cooling wisps of breeze tickling his skin. Today—like every other Florida summer day—promised to be a hot one. Christian was glad to be up and about before the heat and humidity settled in.

Christian, though, had risen with a purpose. As he walked, he carefully studied the beach. In the sand, he noted the footprints of sea birds and the crazy scuttle marks of fiddler crabs. He came across a thin trail left by a skink—a small lizard with a bright blue tail—as it had dragged its tail across the sand. And he also observed the criss-crossings of thousands of shoe, foot, and paw prints left by Palm Beach residents and their trusty canine companions the previous evening.

About half a mile from where he started, though, Christian suddenly stopped. In the sand, he spotted two rows of tiny, parallel indentations leading toward the water. They were tracks—sea turtle tracks.

Like a detective, Christian followed the tracks back to their source high on the beach. He sifted through an empty turtle nest, but found nothing. Then, he followed more tracks along the edge of a retaining wall. Finally, under a plant called a sea grape, he discovered what he was looking for.

"Hi little guy," Christian said, kneeling down. Trapped in the roots of the sea grape, a baby loggerhead sea turtle—the size of

a bar of hand soap—squirmed to get free. Christian untangled the turtle and held it in the palm of his hand. The turtle blinked and stared up at Christian. It moved its flippers once or twice, but it had been weakened by hours of struggling, trying to find its way to the sea. If it had remained stuck in the sea grape's roots, the Florida sun surely would have killed it by sunset. Today, though, good fortune shined down on the turtle. With great care, Christian lowered the turtle into a plastic bucket and smiled. "Another turtle rescued," he thought. "Another job well done."

During the past seven years, Christian had rescued over 15,000 baby loggerhead sea turtles. Every nesting season, he'd been hauling himself out of bed before dawn to patrol a five-kilometer (three-mile) stretch of beach near his house. Seven years earlier, he never imagined the turtles would become such an important part of his life.

> Trapped in the roots of the sea grape, a baby loggerhead sea turtle—the size of a bar of hand soap—squirmed to get free....It moved its flippers once or twice, but it had been weakened by hours of struggling, trying to find its way to the sea.

Christian spent his early years growing up on a farm in Maryland. "One of the major things that sticks out in my mind," he said, "was constantly being surrounded with animals: cows, bulls, chickens, horses, cats, dogs, and geese. My parents tell me that I was a big favorite of the cows when I was small. Whenever I would get near, they would come over and give my face a lick with their huge tongues. When I got larger, my father permitted me to birth a calf, which involved reaching inside the mother and pulling the baby out. From incidents like these, it's not hard to see how I developed a strong love for animals."

When he was seven years old, Christian and his parents left the farm for a new home in Palm Beach, Florida. Palm Beach couldn't have been more different from Maryland, but Christian embraced his new environment. He especially loved spending time on the beach, where one day, an ordinary beach walk changed his life.

He and his parents were out walking on the beach, looking for shells and other objects the tide had brought in, when Christian spotted a small oval object off to the side. As he approached it for a closer look, his heart sank. It was a dead baby loggerhead sea turtle.

Christian felt terrible. What had caused such a beautiful, innocent creature to die? And how could he prevent other turtles from meeting the same fate?

To find out, Christian called the Florida Department of Natural Resources, which put him in touch with wildlife volunteer Pat Fanucan. All sea turtles are endangered or threatened species, but Pat had a special permit to work with the turtles and to train other sea turtle volunteers. Christian told Pat about his experience finding the dead baby sea turtle and asked if there was anything he could do to help. At eight years old, Christian was by far the youngest person who'd expressed an interest in working with the turtles. But Pat could hear the sincerity in Christian's voice, so she asked him if he would like to go through volunteer training.

"Yes!" he replied.

Under Pat's guidance—and with the support of his parents—Christian began learning all he could about sea turtles and their habits. Pat showed Christian how to locate turtle nests by following the wide tracks of adult sea turtles that had come ashore. These tracks, between two and three feet wide, look as if they are made by a miniature tractor or bulldozer. Pat also showed Christian how to surround each nest with wooden stakes to keep beachgoers from disturbing it.

Pat explained to Christian that turtle volunteers kept a careful watch on the nests that they had found. Turtle eggs take about two months to hatch, but each baby doesn't race for the sea as soon as it is born. It waits for its brothers and sisters to hatch, too. Then, when conditions are right—usually at night—the hatchlings help each other dig out of their sandy birthplace and begin making their way to the ocean. This was when Christian's most important job would begin.

Baby sea turtles face enormous hazards after they are born. They can be eaten by raccoons, birds, and other predators. They can become trapped by debris or get lost trying to reach the ocean. Human development only adds to the problems turtles face.

Scientists believe that one way baby sea turtles find their way to the ocean is by crawling toward the brightest part of the sky. At night, under natural conditions, this is usually over the ocean. In many beach communities, however, people have erected streetlights and other sources of artificial light. These lights confuse many of the turtles. Instead of heading for the sea, the tiny babies crawl toward streets, yards, or bushes. When the sun rises in the morning, the turtles are found far from the ocean, and many die from heat exhaustion or are eaten by predators.

In Palm Beach, some people voluntarily turned off their lights at night during the turtle nesting season. But at the time Christian was doing his work, no laws prevented people from leaving their lights on. Christian's job, Pat explained, would be to patrol the beach each morning to find lost turtles and return them to the sea.

After several weeks of training with Pat, Christian was ready to strike out on his own. From April through October, Christian patrolled a stretch of beach near his home. This was the time when female loggerhead, leatherback, and green sea turtles came ashore to nest. Finding and staking out the new turtle nests proved relatively simple. When it came time for the babies to hatch, however, Christian's job grew quite a bit more complicated.

As he walked along the beach each morning, Christian kept a sharp eye out for baby turtle tracks. When he found some, he followed them backward from the ocean to the nest. He searched all around the nest for babies that had become lost or stuck on their way to the sea. He also examined each nest for babies that may have been trapped under the empty shells of their brothers and sisters. When he chanced upon a live baby, he placed it in a bucket. Then, he reburied any eggs that hadn't yet hatched.

At the end of his daily patrol came the most rewarding part of his duties. He carried his bucket to the water's edge and, one by one, released the baby turtles into the sea, happily watching as they paddled through the Atlantic surf to begin their new lives.

Even at age eight, Christian recognized the importance of his work. However, as he grew older and became more experienced

> Christian felt terrible. What had caused such a beautiful, innocent creature to die? And how could he prevent other turtles from meeting the same fate?

at rescuing the turtles, the job presented him with challenges he hadn't anticipated. One was getting himself out of bed so early, every day, for weeks on end. Another was coming across dead turtles.

"At first," Christian explained, "I would feel pity for the small creatures and wished that they could have experienced more of life. Yet seeing dead baby sea turtles was a daily occurrence so, over time, I became desensitized to it. However, I could never say that about those rare occasions when a dead adult sea turtle would wash up on the beach. That was always a gut-wrenching experience."

Another challenge was coping with the reactions of other people. Most adults in his community supported his work, but Christian found that people his own age weren't always understanding. "My close friends were generally supportive," he explained, "but the majority certainly were not. I was often called names like 'Turtle Boy,' and at times this was difficult to deal with."

Christian did make friends with other, older volunteers and received tremendous support from his parents. "I really owe a lot to my parents, who were an incredible source of encouragement and strength. I know I would not have been able to accomplish anything without them."

As Christian kept saving turtles, year after year, his work began to attract more and more attention. In part because he was the youngest person ever to receive a permit to work with the turtles, radio and television stations began seeking him out for interviews. His story appeared in books, magazines, and newspapers, including the *Miami Herald, Chicago Tribune,* and *National Geographic World Magazine.* He also received a number of awards and honors for his conservation efforts.

When he was fifteen years old, Christian received what was perhaps his greatest honor: he was invited to the United Nations headquarters in New York City. Serving as a representative for the United States, he described his turtle activities to over 2,000 students from seventy-six countries. This experience inspired Christian and reinforced his dedication toward protecting sea turtles and the environment.

"While there," he recalled, "I had a sense of hope that the serious problems affecting our earth might be corrected. Whether it's in trying to help our environment, sharing love with others, curing the sick, or aiding the poor, there are many caring people in the world."

Christian continued to do his turtle patrols during junior high and high school. Throughout this time, he kept a "turtle diary" of his activities and observations. He also gathered data that biologists used to learn more about sea turtle biology and behavior. All the while, Christian studied hard at school, played basketball, and pursued his interest in computers. Christian graduated from high school in 1995 as the valedictorian of his class. That fall, he enrolled at Princeton University, where he is now finishing up a degree in philosophy.

A devout Christian—in faith as well as name—he now studies religion and philosophy as ardently as he once worked for turtles. His turtle work, though, has played a pivotal role in shaping his feelings about the world and the role of humans in it.

"I have serious reservations about all forms of biological exploitation," he explained. "To manipulate the world for our own ends is in some sense to pridefully take control of something that is not ours in the first place."

Others, religious or not, agree. Since Christian left Palm Beach, in fact, the city has created regulations that prohibit lights that shine directly onto the beach during the sea turle nesting and hatching seasons. Since the new regulations went into effect, far fewer baby turtles have become lost and stranded. It is another step in our development as human beings—a step that Christian and many other volunteers helped pioneer for us all.

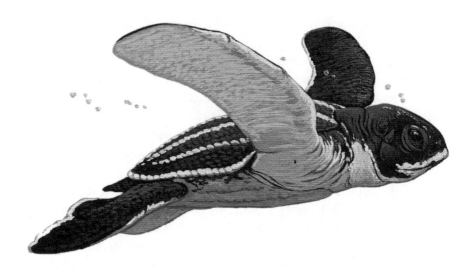

SAVING THE SATIN BOWERBIRD

Sam Madeley, Shannon Bryce, Hannah Gash, and Bree Delian grew up in the small community of Nimbin, which lies in the northeast corner of New South Wales, Australia. The children—all twelve years of age—attended schools in Nimbin or nearby Tuntable Falls, a hilly country of farms and subtropical rain forest. When they weren't busy with school, the children loved to roam through the countryside, enjoying and observing nature, especially wildlife. One of their favorite wildlife neighbors was the satin bowerbird.

Male satin bowerbirds are famous for building U-shaped constructions called "bowers" out of twigs, grasses, and other objects. They use these bowers to attract and court the females they hope to mate with. The bowerbirds are especially fond of decorating their bowers with man-made blue objects. They steal blue clothespins, plastic toys, marbles, and other blue prizes from peoples' backyards and garbage. Biologists believe that these blue objects help the males coax the females to the bowers.

One day, Hannah went out walking and decided to check out a bower near her home. When she reached the bower, however, a sad sight greeted her. Instead of a male actively courting females, she found the small, lifeless body of a bowerbird with a blue plastic ring around its neck. The ring—from a milk bottle top—had slipped around the bird's neck and choked it. Alarmed by her discovery, Hannah asked her friends to check other local bowers for the blue rings. The results were startling. Almost every bower contained at least one of the milk bottle rings.

Hannah, Shannon, Bree, and Sam decided to get together and do something about it. First, they put up posters to alert local residents of the problem. The posters urged people to not buy products with the blue rings or to cut the rings before throwing them away. Once the group started publicizing the plight of the bowerbirds, other concerned residents stepped forward with their own stories about seeing bowerbirds trapped by the deadly blue milk tops. Realizing that the problem was far more widespread than they had thought, the group decided to contact the milk company.

Hannah wrote a formal letter describing the bowerbird death she had witnessed and sent it to Norco, the milk company that used the blue bottle tops. The other students also wrote letters and urged their parents and friends to do the same.

The milk company quickly responded. Norco's group manager, Don Maughan, told the group that his company had not been aware of the problem with the blue tops. After learning about the bowerbird deaths, the company decided to replace the blue tops with white ones. The effect was dramatic. Norco alone had produced 13 million blue bottle tops each year. After they switched to white tops, the number of blue rings in the bowers dropped dramatically.

When the media learned about the story, Mr. Maughan was interviewed on national television, and his words motivated other milk companies to also change the color of their milk tops. People throughout Australia began to search out blue tops from other products and convince companies to change the tops so they wouldn't harm wildlife.

For helping to protect the satin bowerbird, the Nimbin youths received the Greening Australia Award, and Shannon was invited to advise the New South Wales government on environmental issues. But most importantly, by getting other children and adults involved, the students not only protected a species, but raised environmental awareness throughout Australia. As Mr. Maughan, explained, "When something like this happens, it really shows kids that the world is in their hands."

SECRETS OF THE
EARTH

Twelve-year-old Aika Tsubota and her mother stood outside and gazed up at the night sky. Where they lived, in the remote town of Shimane in western Japan, few streetlights interfered with the light from the stars. Tonight, Aika could see the Milky Way, which looked like thousands of grains of shining sand flung across the sky.

Aika stared at the stars for a long time. Then she turned to her mother and said, "I feel big—like the universe. It's as though I'm one with it."

Indeed, Aika felt a special connection with the universe, Earth, and all life. A tall, healthy girl, she loved walking through the woods, exploring the different faces of nature. She had a special interest in history and often asked her father to take her to ancient burial grounds, where she spent hours studying monuments and inscriptions. She expressed her love for the world in her hearty laugh and, in particular, through her art.

Aika began drawing when she was two years old. By the age of five, she was studying art books and copying the cartoon figures from comic books. Soon, she began creating her own characters and stories, making her own comic books, and sharing them with her delighted classmates.

As she grew older, Aika became more and more aware of the environment and the need to protect it. She often went walking with her grandmother to pick up trash in their neighborhood. When she was ten years old, she decided to write her autobiogra-

phy. In it, she wrote, "I would like to become an Earth that is powerful, gentle to cradle, and fosters all of the lives on it."

In September, at the beginning of Aika's second semester in sixth grade, her teacher assigned each student a project of his or her choice to complete before the winter break. Aika decided to do what came naturally: create a comic book. But this comic book would be very different from her others. This one would teach people to care about the world she loved.

Aika set about creating three main characters: the planet Earth, a young boy named Eiichi, and Rumi, a young girl who looked a lot like Aika. In the story, Rumi checks out a book called *Secrets of the Earth* from the local library. When the children open the book, out pops Earth, shouting "Hi there!"

Earth proceeds to teach the two children about the planet's history, as well as explain the water and carbon cycles, photosynthesis, food chains, soil chemistry, weather circulation, and other

> Aika stared at the stars for a long time. Then she turned to her mother and said, "I feel big—like the universe. It's as though I'm one with it."

natural wonders. Earth also shows the two children the many ways in which people have damaged the planet, from oil spills to destroying the ozone layer to cutting down rain forests.

After hearing all of this, Eiichi and Rumi ask Earth, "What can we do to help?" In the last part of Aika's book, Earth tells the children how people can work together to protect the planet. Earth describes how countries can create international laws to protect plants and animals, as well as the everyday things people can do, such as recycling, carpooling, and conserving water.

Aika worked furiously on her project, often drawing late into the night until her mother insisted that she go to bed. She checked out dozens of books on nature and the environment and carefully crafted each page of her comic book so that it was fun, accurate, and easy to understand. Her friends asked her to ride bikes with them or go to the movies, but Aika could think of nothing except her book.

Secrets of the Earth took Aika almost two months to complete, and she proudly handed it to her teacher in late December. Just hours after turning it in, however, Aika suddenly came down with a severe headache. Her parents rushed her to the hospital, but she never recovered. On the morning of December 27, 1991, Aika died of a cerebral hemorrhage.

Devastated by their loss, Aika's parents, family, and friends thought about what they could do to honor her memory and passion toward life. Aika's parents decided to bind *Secrets of the Earth* and give a copy to each of her classmates and teachers.

Inspired by this idea, others decided to spread Aika's message to children throughout Japan and around the world. A group called the Foundation for Global Peace and Environment began publishing *Secrets of the Earth* and distributing it to schoolchildren in Japan. Teachers, students, and parents enthusiastically embraced the book, and it became a textbook in many schools.

Encouraged by this success, the foundation translated the book into Chinese, English, and Arabic and started a Secrets of the Earth Aika club in Japan. Later, Aika's story and book were adapted into a play that was performed over 100 times. Television stations also ran special programs that talked about Aika, her book, and her life.

In 1993, Aika's parents traveled to Beijing, China, to receive the United Nations Environment Programme's Global 500 Roll of Honour Award on behalf of their daughter. They also presented copies of *Secrets of the Earth* to hundreds of other children who attended international children's conferences in other parts of the world.

Since then, the foundation and the Aika Club have organized environmental seminars for adults and symposiums for children. They have sent young delegates to environmental children's conferences all over the world. One, held in Aika's hometown of Shimane, attracted over 400 delegates from nineteen countries.

The Foundation for Global Peace and Environment has continued to publish and distribute Aika's book. In addition to the original four languages, the book has been translated into French, Korean, Vietnamese, German, and Thai. Over 400,000 copies have been distributed throughout the world.

All of these activities would have pleased Aika. Shortly before she died, someone asked her what she thought about when she was working on *Secrets of the Earth*. She wrote down her reply: "The most important thing is for people to stop thinking they can't do anything just because they are only one individual. If everybody thought that way, planet Earth really would be doomed! If everybody pitches in, I know we can turn this planet into a beautiful place."

CONCLUSION:
Taking Action

If this book offers any single lesson, it is that there are as many ways to help the environment as there are people to pitch in. Each person can find his or her own unique way to contribute. Here's how you can get started:

1) Pick an issue close to your heart, one that you especially care about. The more you care, the more effective you will be and the more rewarding your efforts.

2) Start with a manageable, local project. Although global issues aren't out of reach, local issues are often more accessible and can yield faster results. Look around you. Could your community use more bike lanes or a better recycling program? Perhaps more trees could be planted or a local stream cleaned up? Tackling smaller projects will build your confidence and prepare you for bigger issues.

3) Join forces. Involve others in your cause or join others in theirs. Check out environmental groups with local chapters. Such groups often work on projects that take only a day or two each year. If you have more time, you can do more projects.

4) Remember that changing course is fine. It may take more than one attempt to find a project that's right for you.

Whatever path you choose, there are plenty of resources available. One of the best information sources these days is the internet. Many environmental groups—such as the Rainforest Action Network (www.ran.org) and the Jane Goodall Institute's Roots and Shoots organization (www.janegoodall.org), a worldwide environmental and humanitarian program for youth—have websites with basic information and links to other sites. A good place to start is Action For Nature's website, www.actionfornature.org. Many activist groups also have literature they can send you, and don't forget to check with government agencies that deal with environmental issues. All of these groups can be a gold mine of information.

Every step you take will make a difference. Today, our planet faces many serious problems. The courage and determination of people like you will turn things around and create a positive future for us all.

List of Illustrations

Page 83: Palm Beach, Florida
Page 86: leatherback sea turtle
Page 88: satin bowerbird
Page 91: Aika Tsubota with Rumi and Eiichi
Page 104: toad
Front cover: little blue penguin
Back cover: loggerhead sea turtle

About
Action for Nature

Action for Nature (AFN) is a USA environmental education organization based in San Francisco. Our purpose is to foster a respect and affection for nature through personal action. We are particularly interested in encouraging young people to learn and care about nature. We are doing this by producing this book, maintaining a website for young people to exchange environmental news and information, and presenting a nature action program for schools.

AFN started in Assisi, Italy, the home of St. Clare and St. Francis, the patron saint of ecology and nature. There, conservationists B Shimon Schwarzschild, Maria Luisa (Marisa) Cohen, and others successfully fought to protect the songbirds being slaughtered by hunters. Through their action, the hunting of songbirds has been banned in Assisi. These wild birds are now protected and fill the air with their beautiful sounds.

Schwarzschild's nature protection efforts in Assisi and elsewhere convinced him that each individual acting for nature can make a profound difference in the health of the Earth. He founded the Assisi Nature Council/USA, later renamed Action for Nature, to inspire others to carry out their own environmental initiatives. The stories collected and presented in this book by AFN are proof that young people can be successful in restoring the Earth.

You are invited to exchange stories and messages about nature activities! Visit our young people's website, www.actionfornature.org, or write to us at:

Action for Nature
2269 Chestnut Street, Suite 263
San Francisco, CA 94123 USA
email: action@dnai.com

About the Author

Sneed B. Collard III is the author of more than two dozen books, including *Animal Dads; 1,000 Years Ago on Planet Earth; Our Wet World;* and *Monteverde: Science and Scientists in a Costa Rican Cloud Forest.* He received his B.S. in marine biology from the University of California, Berkeley, and his M.S. in scientific instrumentation from the University of California, Santa Barbara. He began writing as a way to educate others about biology and the environment, which eventually led to a full-time writing career.

Sneed believes that the biggest threat to the environment comes from overpopulation. To help ensure that everyone has access to safe family planning, he raises money for Planned Parenthood and donates money to other groups working on this issue. Sneed is also concerned about the spread of exotic species, which are plants and animals that are introduced to new places where they have a negative effect on the environment. He has even written a book about this subject, *Alien Invaders: The Continuing Threat of Exotic Species.*

Sneed currently lives in Missoula, Montana, with his border collie, Mattie. When not writing, he can usually be found traveling and speaking to children and educators about writing, science, and protecting the environment. To learn more about Sneed, visit his website at www.author-illustr-source.com under "Montana."

About the Illustrator

Carl Dennis Buell has been a freelance natural science illustrator for the past twenty years. His drawings and paintings have appeared in books and magazines, as well as at zoos and museums nationwide. Having lived in the American West for most of his adult life, he recently returned to rural upstate New York—in the area he was born and raised—where he now has a studio.

Acknowledgments

Thank you to the young people who appear in these stories, their family members, teachers, friends, and organizational representatives, without whom this book could not have been written.

Donors:

Deep thanks to Marion Rockefeller Weber, Evelyn Ballard de Ghetaldi, Mary M. Griffin Jones, William R. Kimball, Stephen and Julia Kimball, Dr. Jess A. Shenson, Dr. Ben Shenson, Alan and Adrienne Scroggie, and the many others who gave so generously.

Volunteer writers, editors, and researchers:

Lilli Ferguson, Sami Iwata, Bethany Baugh, Charles C. Temple, Lou Satz, Jean La Pez, Chris La Manna, Tansy Mattingly, John Harrison, Lorri Mon, Deanna Toy, Traci Grundy, Amy Carroll, Lisa Jones, Jennifer Squires, Julienne Vulin, Mim King, Dede Hapner, Sarah Skaggs, Beryl Kay (coordinator)

Action for Nature Board of Directors:

Bethany Baugh, Evelyn Ballard de Ghetaldi, Mary M. Griffin Jones, Beryl Kay, B Shimon Schwarzschild (founder), Alan and Adrienne Scroggie, Charles R. Temple, David Yamakawa

Action for Nature Board of Advisors:

Dr. Albert Baez, David Brower, Ruth Gottstein, Dr. Sidney Holt, Huey Johnson, William Whalen

Representatives of the following organizations for story sources, validation of information, and encouragement:

Earth Island Institute (USA), California Academy of Sciences (USA), World Conservation Union (IUCN) (Switzerland), Assisi Nature Council (Italy), Wildlife Clubs of Kenya, National Museums of Kenya, The Quill Hedgehog Club (England), Kiwi Conservation Club (New Zealand), Student Conservation Corps (USA), National Commission for Wildlife Conservation and

Development (NCWCD) (Saudi Arabia), Nimbin High School (NSW, Australia), Massachusetts Audubon Society (USA), BBC Blue Peter Program (England), Young Europeans' Environmental Research Program (Germany), Foundation For Global Peace and Environment (Japan)

Heyday Books:

Malcolm Margolin, Rebecca LeGates, Julianna Fleming, Kathleen Meengs, Rina Margolin